Terminal Leave

poems by

F.S. Blake

Finishing Line Press
Georgetown, Kentucky

Terminal Leave

To Darron Wright and Gaz Crittenden,
two veterans who wrote their books just in time.

ACKNOWLEDGMENTS

As You Were: The Military Review, Vol. 4: "I Didn't Keep a Diary," "Fire"
As You Were: The Military Review, Vol. 5: "One Lone Soul"
Oddball Magazine: "FOB"
Literary Juice Magazine: "Sunset Cigar"
Line Of Advance: " 2Jan," "Flounder," Footing"
The Literary Yard: "Deer Tick"
Eskimo Pie: "For Kelly"

Publisher: Leah Maines
Editor: Christen Kincaid
Cover Art and Design: Mark Babcock, Deeds Publishing LLC
Author Photo: Justin Smith

Printed in the USA on acid-free paper.
Order online: www.finishinglinepress.com
also available on amazon.com

Author inquiries and mail orders:
Finishing Line Press
P. O. Box 1626
Georgetown, Kentucky 40324
U. S. A.

Table of Contents

Railhead

Giant steel discs lubricated by industrial oil
mimic the soldiers executing through toil

sunrise not fresh and new
but old and tired
like a long stretched out night you once knew

Making a transition from static to moving
leaving the base for a new exotic place
lots of motion and missions to get done
young untried hearts ready for proving

Cold and bulky gloves blunt manual agility
frozen fingers fight dumb metal of chains and hooks and bolts
the first step in a long odyssey unfolded
it may look right and done
a whole year left to prove each man's ability

New Bullets

In the prior days of training and falsified eager anticipation
our young minds yearned for war
we cleaned and polished and readied
never thinking it could lead to more

Our guns were called weapons
and they sat as casual anchors of responsibility
never to be left alone
trophies of future veteran promises

When it was time to shoot
to zero in and validate your aim
each round was counted
and recounted in an organized game

Not one could go missing
not even the brass
these were precious and deadly
better bet your ass

Our ration of ammo was how we grew up
one lost bullet we knew
could shut down a range
or disband a brotherly crew

so each one was measured by hand
and watched with military precision

until we went to war

and then on our first day
in a tent in the desert
we were issued our invasion ammo

with careless speed and gluttonous greed
we stuffed our pockets and filled stiff pouches
more than could be missed or counted
whole new bullets flying
like dishes of candy passed to greedy children

Welcome to battle
take as much as you want
or as much as you'll need

I Didn't Keep a Diary

I didn't keep a diary because it was too late to start
So much had already happened
how could I start a work and skip the beginning
I sacrificed capturing the rest of the war for the sake of a few weeks
Those first sunsets saw what may be our last generation of great invaders
We drove to a border and cut through it
we crossed from the world of training into a country belonging to real
    people
Those first few weeks we fought a real army
we launched missiles at tanks
we followed a book

The mission was accomplished
so we moved into an abandoned schoolhouse in between attacks
The war was young and our true enemy wasn't born yet.
I sat down to write but how could I
the depth of a few weeks without running water made my memory too
    cloudy
I couldn't recall the amazing detail I felt I needed
So I didn't

Fire

Campfire of putrid waste
a half barrel of burning fuel and fertilizer
On the surface it's the worst job
The most demeaning statement of your worth

But it's also a pause from the war
a moment in quiet reflection
an inward journey to escape outward smells

does burning shit denote a clear lack of plan?
does it even make sense to do?

Probably not

Convoy

Prolonged drudgery basted in ever present fear

simple tasks like grocery shopping or delivering mail

turned into a war and a mission of life or death

Drivers, passengers, fighters, and more

glued together in a frequency hopping train of common thought

undulating forward and inching slowly together

snaking through a babylonian terror scape

A sitting moving target

for folks that don't want our version of their future

Like predators going after a heard

chances are they can only get one

War Smells Like

A fine dust kicked up by a vehicle in your face
A diesel generator puffing thick waste
Smoke from a fire of brush or trash

Or rubber and plastic all military issue

War smells like all these things and more

Each nasal offensive a reminder of distance and danger

War smells like sweat boiled down to invisible salt lines
Like boots that never get a break

Or blood like iron from a good fishing trip

That's what war smells like

And it stinks

Shrapnel

Hot jagged fragment of post functional form
Splinter sent shooting with erratic force movies can't capture
Explosive will propelling you away from where you started
The heat and impact and grief has bent and contorted you beyond repair
No chance of fitting you back into place now
Flying on a mission to stop a vehicle, mangle a foot, or halt a resolute heart

I feel like you now

Because since we met
In the hot Arabic dry space between two ancient emerald rivers
I'm changed in a way I can't explain

My heart and mind can't fit back into their pre detonation shape
Rugged and craggy and out of place
I don't fit, look different, and can hurt you if you aren't lucky
People avoid the damage I cause
Sent soaring away from the place I knew and belonged, never to fit back

Walking
Human
Shrapnel

FOB

FOB is just a fancy name
for a burned out building or an old abandoned schoolhouse
To some it seems forward like those in the rear or back home
but to our newly minted veteran in the making perspective
it doesn't feel that way at all
it seems perfectly right here, neutral
like sweet, sound, safety, wrapped in America's blanket
A ruck-sack flop at the end of a search
A hot meal of sorts
Mail for some
The only break from a war with no front.
when we leave our resting place
woken by mortars and spurred by young attack lust
We put our team in gear
and shift into pure forward

Sudden Stop

I said keep going because I hoped everything was fine
but the Major and the driver swung us around on a crowded foreign
    highway
previously a long expandable tan snake
now a convoy doubled back on itself like an unnatural beast or a broken
    leg
one vehicle stopped
our interpreter started screaming and ran away
Power lines sparked on the ground
traffic stopped and pedestrians either ran or gawked

We pretended to clear a few houses because that was our job
no one was there, just families
by the time we got back to the scene a helicopter landed and gave birth to
    a stretcher
his foot looked ok but it wasn't
good spirits

The bird left and dust fell quickly
it was thirty minutes since the non-movie blast
I walked the length of the scene and found a small crater
inside it were pieces of jagged metal
I picked one up
it was still burning hot

Terminal Leave

Hours of restless convoy daydreams
Anticipation's voltage a constant power source

Whirring into motion the mind's ability to escape

Transcending mechanized journeys through ancient orchards

First class ticket to sweet home's excess and colors of wanton civilian
    gluttony

Nose shut off to real world smells of sweat, diesel fuel, and dust

Buried roadside danger traded for distant thoughts of loved ones,
and the soldiers longing for a break in the action.

Sweet sleeps ugly half sister, the monotonous drone of first world
tire tracks burning rubber through policy gaps and
            powerpoint confusion draws eyes half closed

Head jerking and bobbing over rough road memories and new found
    regrets

No time left for the undone, a sleepy mix of veteran's remorse and school
    kid hopes.

Radios clicking and popping, vehicles roll on in silent soul black out.

A half dream so real
your oxygen traded for fear
deep marathon gasping breaths
For a friend who's died
Futile surrogate pulmonary attempts
Giant pools of bright boy's blood
Sucking chest wound of guilt and sorrow

The only escape- to not wake up

Sunset Cigar

Like a slow burning fuse to a well-armed sleep bomb

I mark the end of another day alive

Solitary peace breaks the disfigured symmetry of insurgency

And personal holy incense wafts up from my corner of Babylon

I pause and reflect into future veteran mirrors of awe

amazed at what I've seen and been asked to do

I quietly apologize for my own brand of torture

I secretly dissect my mission and mandate

If I pause too long

my mind drifts to the place I came from

Purple mountain majesties of home and love

yearning for foods gone by and trifles of non-war neighborhoods

So I don't

I just quietly puff and stare

and hope I make it to another

sunset cigar

Spear

There is a contempt that grows
the farther away you get from the action
each degree gone from the enemy creates room and comfort
it manifests itself in phrases like
"think it's bad here... you should have been in ____"
everyone looks down on everyone
distance creates dilution of experience
except for those who are in that one spot
they live in the place others only talk about
to observe war is like a pair of scissors cutting a paper clean
to those in the spot the image is magnified
not a clean cut
but actually tiny fibrous strands being ripped apart
they see and live each decision
cause a tear in the fabric of a place they weren't invited to
Hate the people in the rear
because they don't know
and don't have to

Hot Desert Sands

Low palm covered date plantation
Lights orchestrate in the distance like a night at sea
And still, silent buoys mark navigation channels for the donkeys of
    commerce and the taxis of fisherman

Nighttime at war

 A false calm engineered into each sun cycle
Breaking the violence of Mesopotamian heat
And cooling the heels of ancient disputes

Soft river breezes wrap their misty fingers around worn desert
    branches

And stray dogs wake up for the night shift

Stars so bright the night sky dj serves up cool musical hits beyond the
    top ten list.
Deep celestial tracks show, amazing new world clarity

And soldiers wait for dawn.

2Jan

There were loud explosions in a nearby distance
So I grabbed some war things and opened a door
Urgently swept into a tide of action and anger
that dropped us into the back of a thick armored beast

We roared out to a foreign road
A war machine coping with pre weekend rush hour
and we pushed our way to wherever someone said to go
Weapons ready and revenge well loaded

We roamed ancient orchards looking for evidence
that attackers had fired at us from there
we found only farmers and poverty and sweat
a perfect calculus of despair

Their lobs had poked at our temporary home
but when we looked for them now
all drones, and satellites and technological dominance
couldn't solve for their babylonian simplicity

We trudged about, ruining boots and moods
postured with trained arrogance and power
then we loaded back up
and rolled on tracks of futility
back to our violated safe place

It wasn't till we got home
and we saw our leader toss his helmet through a plate glass
window
that we realized an unheard radio broadcast
bore the news of our new forever pain

"Eric is dead"

For Kelly

Northernmost palm tree
Front line troop of tropical expansion
Sweet Southern dreams floating into dormant Northern hibernation
Bolstered by hopes of rope and soil technology
An out of place missionary preaching tales of soft Gulf Stream breezes
    and salty sways of Tradewind kisses
How did you get so far North?
Set as a monument to our Post-Modern nomadic job wandering
A dropped waypoint reminder of happier times and sunnier climes

I want to wrap you in a blanket
And sing away frozen harshness and the salty roads biting breath
I'd wipe away icicles and snow from your proud green fans of palm
    ancestry
You watch as your left and right neighbors fade into modest
foliage drops and red leaf uselessness
You may not belong here, but your beauty transcends latitudinal confines

And on a cold December morning
Your sacrifice and deep-rooted disregard for your own struggles
Gives me hope
That Winter won't last forever
And Summer will be here soon

You stand as proof that people and things are here for a reason
and they can evolve past their origin to fit any season

Buoy

Lifted up or anchored down?
Square top or round? The difference is meaningful I seem to think

You silently mark the path that should be free from danger
But how do I know
I have to trust you—FORCED to trust your mocking bell and dim light
What if you've made a mistake and drifted off your mission?

By the time I learn you are a second rate identifier I'll be in trouble

Prop down, sandbar reunion

Don't let me down... lift me up

Flounder

I break the laws of skeletal nature
to me symmetry is not important

My offset eyes focus on a mean world of hooks and crooks above
life doesn't get much lower than me
I'm on the bottom of the world's belly
so threats to me are more narrowly defined

but they still exist
so I skirt about in a ruffle of sand and hypnotic fin ripples
I can't run and fight
I don't triple or homer, my swings produce mostly gounders
So I'll lay low in the flats
and hope I make it through another Cape Cod night
with all my fellow slim flounders

One Lone Soul

Bobbing oscillation on each incoming wave
Infinite blue ocean ahead transforms
Optimistic goals into the futility of expanse

One lone soul fighting ebbs and tides not for progress but experience

Hundreds watch from a packed summer beach
Sun seekers slathered in modes of sun protection
So close to the destination of their hundred mile journey

They cry and sweat and burn
In beach chair safety

All their eyes trained on

One lone soul

Deer Tick

Like the herpes of the woods you seek to infect my life and vacation
I'm not your intended prey and I am not out looking for you

You take advantage of my desire to frolic and play
your presence makes me a prisoner of our own beautiful beach house

Unknown to me you seek an unsanctioned symbiosis
Claiming your right to jump a few links in the food chain

Go pick on a deer or a dog or something that won't mind
I cringe at the thought of you engorged on my blood

A tenacious squatter you require minor surgery to remove
A civil war aid kit of tweezers and matches and pain

Head first you drink all you can of my life in stolen gulps
you get fat on me and I may not even notice

somehow when I flush you down the toilet after I've uncovered your plot
I know your life will still continue and your hunt will not end

Waiting quietly with endless insect patience
your mind blank with blood lust

You pause for opportunity to simply brush by
a silent ride of survival in a flea eat dog world

Footing

Everything felt right with my connection to the world
legs strong and proud held their ground firm
and steely eyes in squinting sun protection mode
wasted no time looking down

I could see as far as the earth would let me
calm running acres of oceanic blanket
mixed tonal resonance of every shade of water
lifted boats and plans and people on the horizon

The sea was warm
it welcomed my toes into its vast salty adventure
and strong or gentle waves pushed against my shins
the water rushed past me

I didn't move
no desire to wade deeper or retreat to the dry grainy beach
but the world paid no respect to my position and made me move
by removing every fleck beneath my heavy feet

I found myself standing on flimsy pillars and worn out plateaus
erosion had found a way
half tempted to stick my ground
I gave way to the power that stole my footing

Shuttered

We stole a Summer weekend from the Fall
and observed a brief stall of winters' trudge
like an encore sung well after the last set
a quick reprieve from a benevolent judge
Our early Spring inverse brings a tan
to our pumpkins and gourds
And our beach shadows were longer and thinner
than their July cousins
Sunburn beneath our fleeces
we depart the island
and leave it
shuttered

F.S. Blake is a Bronze Star decorated U.S. Army Veteran. He is a published photographer, traveler, advanced SCUBA diver, philanthropist, entrepreneur, and proud husband and father. He has poems published or forthcoming in *O-Dark-Thirty, As you Were: The Military Review, The Wrath-Bearing Tree,* and *Line of Advance.* His poetry career began during his sister's wedding.